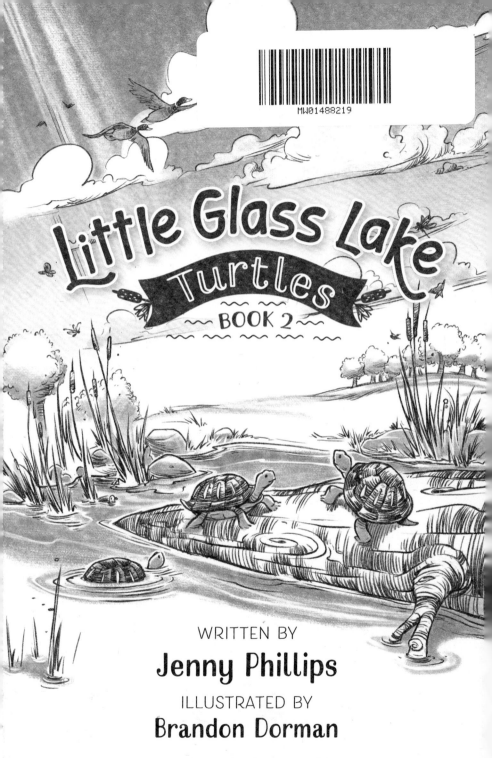

Little Glass Lake

Turtles

BOOK 2

WRITTEN BY
Jenny Phillips

ILLUSTRATED BY
Brandon Dorman

TABLE OF CONTENTS

Chapter 1

Holly breathed in the smell of freshly mowed grass and marveled at dewdrops sparkling in the sun.

Spring was in full bloom at Little Glass Lake. Orange poppies nodded in the breeze, and the apple trees in Holly's yard were covered with thousands of tender green leaves.

Holly, her mom, and her brother Henry sat around a big table on the back porch. A stack of pancakes and a stack of books sat on the table.

"I love doing school outside in spring!" Holly bubbled.

"Me too!" Holly's mom
smiled.

"Me three!" Henry said.

"Well," said Holly's mom, "now that we have prayed, let's dig into these pancakes."

Breakfast, history, and math whizzed by as the twittering birds filled the air with songs.

After chores and piano practice, the sun had gotten quite hot, so Holly

curled up on the couch
with a book to read.

With a playful smile
on his face, Henry walked
into the room with his
hands behind his back.

"Have you finished all
of your chores?" he asked.

"Yep!" Holly said as she
closed her book.

Henry pulled a beach
towel from behind his

back and tossed it to her.

"Well, then! Want to go swimming in the lake? It's finally warm enough. Mom said we can go today."

In five big leaps, Holly bounced across the room and disappeared through the door as she called, "I'll be in my swimsuit in a jiffy!"

While skipping to the lake next to Henry and her mom, Holly smiled. "I love swimming in Little Glass Lake!"

Mom insisted that Holly wear her life jacket while in the lake until she was a teenager. Because she was eight years old, she had five more years of wearing a life jacket. She didn't love wearing it, but she understood why the rule was important.

As the deep blue sky smiled above them, Holly and Henry ran down their favorite grassy slope by the lake and jumped into the cool water.

Holly's mom laid out a blanket on the grass and sat down to watch the

kids swim and enjoy the
warm spring day.

I feel like a silvery fish,

Holly thought as she swam around in the water.

After a while, Henry and Holly launched their small rowboat into the water and floated around lazily. A little breeze began to ripple the water and dry Holly's wet hair. She closed her eyes and leaned her head back, enjoying both the warmth of the sun and the freshness of the breeze.

Without warning, Henry splashed Holly with an oar.

"Oh! You'll pay for that!" Holly said with a big grin as she began splashing Henry back with her own oar.

Then the oar slid through her wet hands

and plunked into the water. The light breeze had created a gentle current in the lake, and the oar started floating away.

"I'll get it!" Holly called, jumping so quickly from the boat that it rocked wildly and tipped Henry out.

Laughing, the siblings

both swam over to the reeds where the oar had floated. Holly got there first and saw the end of the oar.

She reached for the oar and then jerked her hand back and screamed. There in the reeds she saw a little face with yellow eyes and a slimy brown head staring at her. The head

was in some kind
of dark shell, and
it started hissing at
Holly.

Chapter 2

Forgetting completely about the oar, Holly screamed and began swimming to the shore with such a thrashing and splashing that her mom stood up and called out, "What's wrong? What's going on? Is everything OK, Holly?"

All Holly could think about was that terrible hissing head and those horrible yellow eyes. She swam toward the shore as she never had before, scrambled up the bank, and ran through her yard, screaming all the way.

Once in the house, Holly ran into the living room, grabbed a blanket,

wrapped it around herself, and curled up on the couch.

Holly's mom arrived in the living room out of breath and panting for air.

"Holly! Are you OK? What happened?" she asked between deep breaths. Her mother was clearly alarmed.

"Oh!" Holly wailed. "It

was a little monster. Some horrid thing with a slimy head and beady yellow eyes. Now I can never swim in Little Glass Lake again. Never!"

Hearing all the noise, Holly's dad came out of his office, also alarmed. "Is everything OK in here?"

Fresh tears pooled in Holly's eyes and trickled

down her cheeks.

Henry finally arrived after bringing the rowboat back to shore.

"Oh, did you see it, Henry? Did you see that horrible thing with yellow eyes hiding in the reeds? Some monster has taken over the lake! There are probably dozens of those little things in the water." She shuddered just thinking about it.

"Yes, I saw it," Henry said. "But, Holly, it wasn't a monster. I know what it was."

With interest, Holly sat up. "What was it?"

"It was just a harmless turtle that you scared— that's all. It swam away from me, and I got the oar. Everything is OK. We've never seen a turtle in the lake before. It's kind of neat that we have one!"

Neat? Holly thought. *That is horrible, not neat!*

Holly's dad knelt down beside her and patted her shoulder. "See, it's OK. It was just a turtle. There's no need to be scared."

But Holly was scared!

Oh, how frightening those yellow eyes had seemed to her. She didn't care if the turtle *was* harmless. She thought it was a horrid little thing.

Holly sighed heavily and walked over to the large family room window. Through it Holly could see Little Glass Lake shimmering in the

distance, and one more
tear slid down her cheek.
*I just know I can never
swim there again.*

Chapter 3

A few hours later, sensing that Holly was still scared from seeing the turtle, Holly's mom suggested that she read the *Good and Beautiful Animal Guide* that was all about turtles.

"Have you read that one before?" Mom asked.

Holly shook her head. "No, I've never thought turtles were cute, so I've just never read that guide. And now I never want to read it."

Holly's mom frowned. "Hmmm. Well, let's get your mind on something else, then. Faith's mom texted me a few minutes ago. Faith's last day of school is today, and she wants you to come over and play."

Holly perked up a little. "I'd love to go." She stopped and thought for a few seconds. "Mom, how does Faith do her schoolwork if she is blind, or know what the teacher writes on the board?"

"Those are good

questions, and you should ask her," Mom responded. "Yesterday, I chatted with Mrs. Timms. I asked her what we should know about being friends with someone who is blind. She told me that you should always just ask Faith if you have a question or if you don't know what to do when you are around her."

Holly nodded. "OK. Thanks, Mom."

An hour later, Faith and Holly were sitting at Faith's kitchen table, talking and eating some of Mrs. Timms's muffins. They were delicious, and Holly couldn't wait for the Happy Duck Bakery to open so she could try more of Mrs. Timms's amazing baking.

Holly had just finished her story about the awful turtle, how scared she had been, and how she never wanted to swim in the lake again.

"That does sound scary!" Faith agreed. "But I think it's just because it took you by surprise. Turtles are nothing to be scared of. Surely, you will feel like swimming again soon."

No, I won't, Holly thought to herself, but she

didn't want to say that to Faith. So she changed the subject.

"I wanted to ask you about school. Do you go to a school just for children who are blind?"

"Some blind children do go to that kind of school, but many blind children go to regular schools like I do. I go to an extra class to learn how to read braille. Do you know what that is?"

Holly nodded. "It's raised-up dots that you read with your fingers, right?"

"Right! Well, I go to that class, and then I go to the regular classes. I have a friend named Mrs. Banks who helps me if I have

trouble with anything."

"Do you take your
guide dog, Mac, to school
with you?"

"Oh, I wish I did, but

I can't. I do bring a cane, though."

So many other questions were swirling in Holly's mind, but she didn't want to ask too many questions all at once. She decided to wait for another time to ask.

"Do you want to go see the ducklings?" Faith asked.

"Yes!" Holly responded. "And I'd love to see the pheasant chick, too."

Chapter 4

Holly, Faith, and Mac went into the barn. Holly smiled to see all the ducklings. They had gotten so much bigger.

Mr. Timms was in the barn and waved to Holly. "Come on over, girls. The ducklings are taking their first swim today."

Smiling, Holly watched as Mr. Timms transferred a small group of ducklings from their box to a large, shallow water dish.

Faith dipped her fingers in the water and then stroked one of the ducklings. "This is so fun, Dad! I love raising ducks with you!"

"The water is not very

deep," Holly noted. "They can't really swim in it."

"Not yet," Mr. Timms explained. "They are just under two weeks old, so they don't have their waterproof feathers yet. Also, they don't make their waterproof oil yet."

"Ducks have waterproof oil?" Holly asked.

Mr. Timms nodded.

"Yes, ducks have a gland that makes a waterproof oil. When ducks preen themselves, they take the oil and rub it over their feathers."

Holly giggled as she watched the ducklings splash and play in the water. She described the scene to Faith. "They are so excited to be in the

water for the first time!"

Mr. Timms explained more. "Until the ducklings grow feathers and preen them with oil, I am just getting them used to a little water. We won't allow them to go in the lake for several more weeks."

Holly nodded as Mr. Timms continued.

"Without feathers they also get cold easily, so I will only leave them in the water dish for a few minutes. Then back to the heat plates they go!"

Holly was very interested in the waterproof oil. "I never knew what preening was, but now I know why ducks move their beaks all over their feathers. I see them do that all the time." She paused and tilted her head a little. "Wait— you said the ducklings shouldn't swim in the lake for several weeks, but when the blue-winged teal ducklings hatched, they were in the water within a day!"

"That's right, they were!

In the wild, ducklings get covered by their mom's oil," Mr. Timms replied. "You see, they snuggle up against and under her feathers, which are covered in oil, so they get the oil on themselves and are fine to go in the water."

"Oh!" Holly said, her mouth making a little O

shape. "Ducklings are so interesting," she bubbled. "And I just love listening to their cute little sounds!"

For another hour, Holly and Faith helped Mr. Timms give all the ducklings a chance to try out the water.

When they finally put the last duckling back in its box, Mr. Timms asked,

"Do you want to see the pheasant chick, Holly?"

"Yes!" she exclaimed with a huge smile.

"Then follow me. It's out in the fenced barnyard," Mr. Timms replied with a wave of his hand.

"Oh, won't it get in the lake?" Holly asked as she followed Mr. Timms

through the barn.

With a shake of his head, Mr. Timms explained, "Pheasants can swim, but they don't like to. Your little chick prefers to keep its feet dry."

"Oh, it has feathers," Holly noted when she saw the pheasant walking around. Then, to Holly's surprise, the pheasant started running and took off, flying about ten feet before landing again.

"It can already fly!" Holly gushed.

"I can hear its wings swooshing," Faith said as she clapped her hands together.

"When will your ducklings start flying?" Holly asked Mr. Timms.

"Well," started Mr. Timms, "they won't. They're Saxony ducks, and Saxony ducks don't fly. That is why we'll be able to let them out here in this fenced area. They won't fly out of it."

That made sense to Holly, so she nodded. Then she turned and looked at the pheasant.

"Oh, he's just so cute! When do I get to take him home?" she asked excitedly.

Mr. Timms frowned. "Well—we'd better talk about that, Holly."

Chapter 5

Holly's heart sank. *Mr. Timms wants to keep my pheasant*, she thought.

Letting out a long sigh, Mr. Timms looked Holly in the eyes as he spoke. "You see, keeping a pheasant as a pet is not an easy thing. First, they are not that friendly. They can even be mean."

Holly gulped. "Oh. I don't like mean animals."

"Second, they will fly away unless you clip their wings or keep them under a roof so they can't fly."

Suddenly, Holly realized the pheasant wouldn't be her pet. She tried to hold back the tears forming in her eyes.

"Clip his wings? No, I don't want to do that," she mumbled. "I wouldn't want to stop him from flying, and we don't have a place to keep him that has a roof over it."

Sensing that Holly was upset, Faith put her hand on Holly's arm. "He can be yours for a little while, though—until he flies away," she said, hoping to comfort her friend.

Holly's lip trembled. *I watched that egg hatch. We saved the chick and helped it get food and safety. Now it's just going to fly away and be gone forever?*

Holly couldn't help feeling upset, and Mr. Timms could tell.

"I'll tell you what,

Holly," Mr. Timms offered. "The sun is so warm today, and Little Glass Lake looks so cool and refreshing. How about I take you and Faith swimming? We can go right now. I'm all finished with the ducklings."

It was too much for Holly. She didn't know how to tell Mr. Timms that she was scared of a turtle. But there was no way she could get in the lake, and she was still feeling very sad about the pheasant.

"Maybe another time," Holly mumbled. Turning on her heels, she dashed away. Out of the barnyard she went, down the hill, and into the

grassy fields by the lake.

Running wildly, she suddenly realized that she was breaking the rule about going around the lake by herself. Even though she was staying far from the water, she still felt terrible. *I broke the rule! Oh, I broke the rule!*

She ran even faster, jumping over a log,

dodging through some trees, and trampling over wildflowers. She scared all the ducks by the lake, causing them to fly away with a mighty flapping of wings.

Holly reached her house so out of breath that her mom was alarmed.

"What happened?" Holly's mom asked.

Holly curled up on the couch for the third time that day.

"I broke the rule!" she sobbed to her mom. "I went around the lake by myself, and I'm sooooo sorry! And the pheasant, I guess, is a meanie, and I would be a meanie to clip his wings. And Mr. Timms wouldn't understand about a girl who is scared of a turtle."

Holly could tell her mom didn't fully understand why she was so upset. Holly then found herself wrapped in her mother's comforting arms.

"It's OK, Holly," her mother said as she stroked her hair. "We don't have to talk about it right now. You should calm down first and then tell me all the details."

Chapter 6

The next day was sunny and warm. Holly gazed at the white clouds outside her bedroom window. They looked like fluffy sheep.

Chewing on her pencil, she looked back down at her paper and then started writing again.

After a few minutes, she
set the pencil down and
smiled.

"All done!" she said
to her cat, Daisy, who

only flicked her tail and blinked.

As Holly took the paper to her mother, she thought about the consequence she had been given for going around the lake by herself.

The first part of my consequence—cleaning out my closet—wasn't very fun. It took me a whole hour!

The second part was a little fun, though. I didn't think writing this report would be fun, but it kind of was. I like writing!

Holly found her mother in the kitchen and handed her the report. "Here it is—a two-page report on how rules are a blessing."

Her mother read through the paper and

nodded. "Very good, Holly. I do believe that you want to follow the rules, and I am so glad. Your consequence is finished. You can play for a while before bedtime."

Ding! It was the doorbell.

"I'll get it!" Holly sang as she skipped away.

Flinging the door open,

Holly was surprised to find Mr. Timms standing there, holding an open box. The sun was sending both long shadows and golden shafts of sunlight across the front lawn.

Mr. Timms quickly handed the box to Holly.

"Here you go!" he said. "Instructions are in the box. We have to run, or

we are going to be late for
our plane. Sorry this is
all so last minute. Thank
you!"

Holly was confused. She wondered what was going on as she watched Mr. Timms hop into his car and pull away.

That's strange, Holly thought as she shrugged. Looking down into the box, she saw something move. Holly gasped. She was pretty sure it looked like a . . . turtle!

Quickly, Holly set the box down on the porch and ran right to her mother, who was talking to Henry in the family room.

"It's a . . . it's a turtle!" blurted Holly, interrupting their conversation. "On our front porch! Go see!"

"What?" Henry exclaimed as he dashed to

the front porch. He came back carrying the box, a confused look on his face.

"Oh, don't bring a turtle into our house!" Holly begged.

"But it's for you," Henry said.

"How do you know?"

"There's a note in the box that says, 'Dear Holly, Thank you for taking care of my pet turtle Ziggy.'"

Henry finished reading and looked up at Holly. "A sheet with instructions is taped on the box."

"What?!" Holly gasped. "Mr. Timms just brought his turtle to me without even asking?"

Holly's mom shook her head. "No, he asked me. I

said you would be happy to watch his turtle. It's just a little one."

"Why would you do that?" Holly asked. "You know that I'm scared of turtles."

"That is why I said yes, Holly. I thought that if you could see how cute and harmless turtles can be, you wouldn't be scared of them anymore."

"Oh, Mom!" Holly sniffed, holding back tears. "I don't want to even look at that thing. Please, don't make me take care of it!"

"I'll do it," Henry offered.

"That will be helpful, Henry. Thank you," said Mom.

"Wait!" Holly's eyes widened. "Who is caring for the ducklings and the pheasant chick?"

"Mr. Timms said they hired someone to come twice a day to take care of them," Holly's mom shared.

"I could have done that instead," Holly mumbled with a frown.

"Come on, Ziggy!" Henry said as he took the box out of the room.

"Just keep that thing far away from me!" Holly called after him.

Chapter 7

The next day was the day they went to church, and Holly was extra grateful to get out of the house.

She shook her head as she walked up the hill to the church. *I just can't be comfortable with a turtle in my house. What if it gets loose? It's too bad our lake has to have a turtle, but it's even worse to have a turtle in my house. Still, look at this beautiful day! I'm not going to think about turtles anymore today.*

Wildflowers dotted the hillside. A bluebird cut across the sky and landed on a tree branch.

Like always, golden

morning light poured through the church windows. Holly sang the first hymn joyfully:

I see the stars,
I hear the rolling thunder,
Thy power throughout the Universe displayed!

Right in front of Holly sat a family who was close friends with Holly's family: Mrs. Parkes and

her four-year-old boy, Johnny.

With a smile, Holly watched as Johnny turned around and peeked over the bench. All she could see were his eyes and the top of his head.

Holly gave Johnny a little wave, and then he popped his head down. Up and down went his

head, and a giggle escaped
his lips.

Holly held a finger up
to her mouth, showing

him that he should be
quiet.

Johnny turned around.
Just then, Holly heard
another noise—a groan.
Where did that come from?

Johnny's behavior was
very distracting, so it was
hard for Holly to focus
on the words being said
in the meeting. First, he
untied the bows on the

braids of the girl in front of him and let them fall to the floor.

Holly shook her head and gave Johnny a little frown when he turned around with a grin. Then she made herself focus on the minister's words.

But she couldn't help watching Johnny as he took his snack box and

threw a handful of raisins
into the air. They landed
in a lady's hair.

The lady looked around
and patted her head. She
pulled the raisins out of
her hair, looking confused
and surprised. Johnny
peeked over the bench
again. Holly gave a sharp
shake of her head and
shook her finger at him.

Then there was another
groan, much louder this
time. Some people started
looking around.

With wide eyes, Holly watched as Johnny took the lid off a marker he had found in his mom's bag. The lady in front of him had on a wide-brimmed white hat. Johnny started scribbling on it with the green marker.

Should I do something? Why is Johnny's mom not watching him? Doesn't

she see what is going on?

thought Holly with alarm.

Holly's mom and Henry

saw what Johnny was doing, too, and Holly's mom leaned forward, trying to get Johnny to settle down.

At the same time, Holly noticed that Mrs. Parkes was bent over holding her stomach. When another groan was heard, Holly and her family suddenly realized that the noise was coming from Mrs. Parkes.

Suddenly, the woman slumped over on the bench, not even trying to hold back her groans anymore.

The minister stopped speaking, and everyone began to talk in hushed voices. Holly's dad rushed over to Mrs. Parkes.

"Are you OK?"

"No," Mrs. Parkes said weakly. "Oh! My stomach! It's hurting so badly, I can't stand it. I have such a sharp pain right here." She pointed to her right side.

Mrs. Parkes moaned loudly. "Oh, something is really wrong. Can someone take me to the hospital?"

"I can!" offered a lady sitting next to her.

"And we can watch Johnny," Holly's mom offered.

"Thank you, that would be so helpful," Mrs. Parkes said.

Chapter 8

Johnny was quiet as he walked home with Holly and her family.

When they arrived at Holly's house, Johnny sniffed and stopped on the porch. "I want to go to my house with my mommy."

"I know, dear," Holly's

mom said. "But she is feeling sick, and she is going to get help. I'm sure she will be fine. In the meantime, we can have a lot of fun."

"OK," Johnny said.

He is such a cute little boy, Holly thought as she held his hand and walked into the house.

Johnny wasn't interested

in playing games, or drawing pictures, or even making cookies.

He just sat on the couch holding Daisy. After a while, he fell asleep, and everyone was quiet so he could take a nap.

When the phone rang, Johnny popped up with a start. He listened while Holly's mom talked to the caller. Finally, she hung up and went to sit by Johnny.

"Good news! Your mommy is fine! She had a lot of pain because her appendix burst."

"I don't know what an appendix is," Johnny said, crinkling up his eyes. "But I'm glad she's OK. Is she coming to get me?"

"No, they had to take her appendix out, and now she has to stay in the hospital for at least three days. She said you could stay here."

Little pools of tears formed in Johnny's eyes, and his bottom lip trembled. Holly's heart just about broke to see him so sad.

What can I do to cheer him up? she thought. Nothing came to mind, so she said a little prayer in her heart. Then she had an idea.

"Johnny! Do you remember that we live around a lake? It's called Little Glass Lake, and it's just wonderful. All sorts of animals live around it. Do you want to go exploring with me?"

That worked! Johnny

jumped up, nearly spilling the cat onto the floor.

"Oh, yes! I am really good at exploring."

"I can take you guys," Henry offered.

Holly had always wanted a little brother or sister, and it kind of felt like she had one now—at least for a few days. She held Johnny's hand as they walked across the yard and down to the lake.

The lake shimmered in the afternoon sun. Everything seemed bright and alive. Wildflowers were like splashes of colored paint across the fields. Red and blue birds darted about, and brown-and-green cattails swayed slowly in the breeze.

Johnny clapped his hands for joy when he saw a squirrel, a group of ducks, and a hummingbird.

But then, as they went close to some reeds by the water, Holly saw something that made her heart race: two turtles.

Chapter 9

"Look at the turtles!" Johnny shouted. "My favorite animal!"

"You like turtles?" Holly asked.

"They are the best!"
Johnny said.

Holly had to admit that
the turtles did not look as
scary when they were out
on a log, basking in the
sun.

"They are so cute. Don't
you think so, Holly?"
Henry asked.

"Hmmm, maybe a
little. The turtle I saw in

the water must have been a different kind of turtle," Holly declared.

"No, that is the same kind of turtle. It's a western pond turtle," Henry explained kindly.

"Well, looking at them is different than swimming with them," Holly stated.

"You can swim in this

water?" Johnny asked excitedly. "You can swim with the turtles? Oh, Holly, can you please take me swimming with the turtles?"

"I . . . well . . ." Holly frowned.

Little Johnny clapped his hands and jumped up and down. "Pretty please?" he pleaded.

How can I tell this little boy that I am afraid of swimming in the water with the turtles? He's not afraid, and he's only four!

"We'll see," she said.

"Oh, I really, really hope we can," Johnny gushed.

As the group walked back to the house, Holly noticed dark clouds in the distance. The air was turning colder. There was a flash in the sky far, far away.

Oh, good! Holly thought. *If it's stormy tomorrow, then we can't swim in the lake anyway.*

In the morning, Holly was happy to see that rain was falling.

But Johnny was not

happy with the rain.

"I want to swim with the turtles," he said all morning.

To try and cheer him up, Henry let him hold Mr. Timms's pet turtle Ziggy.

"Here, you can hold him now," Johnny said to Holly after a while.

With a shake of her

head, Holly said, "No, thank you."

After dinner, Holly's mom noticed that Johnny was very antsy and bored.

"Why don't you let Holly read something to you, Johnny?" Holly's mom urged.

But Johnny shook his head. "I don't want to read a book right now," he said with a sigh.

"You love turtles, don't you?" Holly's father asked. "Did you know Holly has a book about turtles?"

Johnny's eyes lit up. "I want Holly to read me *that* book!"

"All right," Holly said with a sigh.

She went into her room and took the *Good and*

Beautiful Animal Guide about turtles from the shelf.

Sitting by Johnny on the couch, she opened the guide and, with another big sigh, began to read.

As she read the book aloud to Johnny, she learned a lot of things about turtles she didn't know before. Many turtles

can live out of the water for a long time. They are very smart animals. When they feel scared, they bury themselves in the mud.

Partway through the book, Johnny said, "Aren't turtles great? God made them, didn't He?"

Holly smiled. "Yes, God made them." Then she thought for a moment.

She had to admit that the facts she had been reading about turtles were very neat. The book didn't say anything about turtles being mean or biting people. That made Holly feel a little better about sharing the pond with turtles.

So she turned to Johnny and said, "I'm not sure.

Maybe turtles are amazing. Maybe they are not. I'm still thinking about it."

The next day turned out to be rainy too. The rain drizzled off and on all day.

After lunch, the wind picked up, and it somehow opened the gate to the chicken coop. Their chickens scattered around the yard, where they scratched at the ground and tugged out worms.

Holly was given the task of watching Johnny while everyone else went to gather the chickens.

Johnny sat down on the couch and sighed. "When can I see my mom again?"

"Soon!" Holly said. "In fact, my mom said you

probably get to go home tomorrow night."

"Tomorrow night! That is sooooo far away," Johnny replied.

Holly looked around the room, trying to think of some way to keep the little boy busy. She spotted a stuffed tiger and said, "Do you want to play Find the Tiger?"

"Sure!" Johnny piped. "How do you play?"

"Well, you go out of the room, and then I hide the tiger. When you come back in, you try to find it."

Find the Tiger was a hit. It seemed that Johnny would never tire of it.

Finally, Holly said, "OK, that's all for now.

I'm going to go make us a snack."

When Holly came back into the room with a tray of cheese and crackers, Johnny jumped up.

"We are going to play Find the Turtle!"

"What do you mean?" Holly asked with concern.

"I wanted to play

another game, so I hid the turtle."

Holly felt alarm and anger rising in her. "Do you mean you hid the real live turtle Ziggy?"

Johnny nodded his head proudly. "Yep! See if you can find him."

"Oh, Johnny!" Holly exclaimed. "You should not have done that."

Chapter 10

Holly calmed down because it looked like Johnny might cry.

"It's OK, Johnny. Just tell me where you hid the turtle."

He pointed to a bookcase, where a stepladder had been placed. "He's on top of the bookcase."

Looking up, Holly saw that Ziggy was indeed on the bookcase. His head was inside his shell. She felt scared that Ziggy might end up falling off.

Oh, I can't let Ziggy get hurt. He's Mr. Timms's pet.

Without remembering that she didn't want to touch a turtle, Holly climbed up the stepladder and took Ziggy in her hands. After she had him safely down, she walked over to the couch, sat down, and held the turtle in her lap.

After a minute, the turtle poked his head out of his shell.

Holly giggled. She realized that his little head

was actually cute, not scary.

"Do you like turtles now?" Johnny asked.

Holly nodded.

Her family was very surprised to see the turtle on Holly's lap when they came in.

The next morning, Holly stirred and then opened her eyes. Johnny was standing there in his swimsuit.

"It's not raining," he said. "Your mom got my swimsuit when she went to my house to get more clothes yesterday. Can we go swimming now?"

With a laugh, Holly got out of bed. "We have to wait until it warms up. We can go after lunch."

Later that morning, Holly and Johnny sat on the living room floor, watching Ziggy crawl around.

"He moves so slow," Johnny said with a giggle.

Just then, the doorbell rang. Holly scooped up the turtle and went to answer it.

Holly was so happy to

find Mr. and Mrs. Timms and Faith on the doorstep.

"We're back!" Faith called when she heard the door open. "How is Ziggy?"

"He's great!" Holly said. "He's right here." She held out Ziggy and placed him in Faith's hands.

At that moment, Gabe came riding his bike down

a dirt trail that led to Holly's driveway.

"Hello!" Gabe called as he set down his bike and ran up to the porch.

"I was thinking it's a great day for swimming. Who wants to go?" he asked.

Mr. and Mrs. Timms looked at Holly, as if remembering what Faith

had told them about
Holly's fear of the turtles
that lived in the lake.

Holly took a deep
breath, looking at the
turtle in Faith's hands.

"I do!" Holly said.

Johnny came running
to the door. "Oh, I do! I
do!"

Faith raised her hand.
"I do too! I'll go change

into my swimsuit!"

Soon, the kids and their parents were at Little Glass Lake. It sparkled as if it were laughing along with the children.

Holly looked across the lake and saw a turtle sunning itself on a big log. *It's OK*, she told herself. *Just as Johnny told me, turtles are amazing animals. Also, they won't come close to me.*

With a flying leap, Holly jumped into the

water and let the coolness rush over her. She called for Johnny to come.

He ran into the water, holding Henry's hand.

Faith, Mr. Timms, and Gabe soon joined them too.

After splashing and playing with the group, Holly floated on her back away from everyone. She listened to the ripple of water around her. She watched the clouds swim by in an endless lake of blue sky. The pair of blue-winged teal ducks, whose nest she had watched over, flew above her, their beautiful wings stretched out in the air.

A smile lit up her face. *I'm glad I changed my*

mind about turtles. They are pretty amazing, and I can see why they would love to live here. Little Glass Lake is amazing too!

Continue the adventures with book 3 of the Little Glass Lake series!

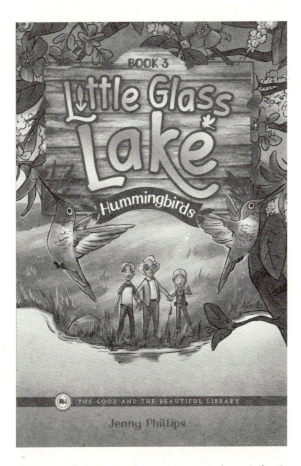

Little Glass Lake Hummingbirds
By Jenny Phillips

goodandbeautiful.com

*Try another Level 2B book from
The Good and the Beautiful.*

Ollie the Ox and Other Animal Tales
By Kathy Leckrone & Shannen Yauger

goodandbeautiful.com

Try another Level 2B book from
The Good and the Beautiful.

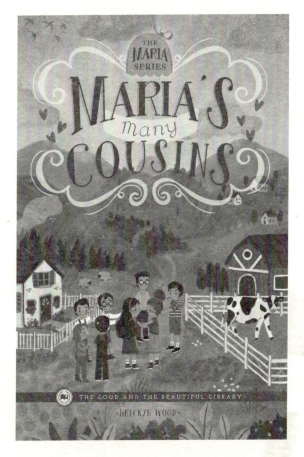

Maria's Many Cousins
By Breckyn Wood

goodandbeautiful.com